An introduction to the printing processes

edited by Michael Barnard

A Pira visual guide

© Copyright Pira International 1994
Reprinted 1996

ISBN 1 85802 080 8

Published by
Pira International
Randalls Road
Leatherhead
Surrey
KT22 7RU
UK

Tel: (+44) (0) 1372 802080
Fax: (+44) (0) 1372 802079
E-mail publications@pira.co.uk
http: //www.pira.co.uk

Typeset in the UK by The Heronwood Press, Medstead, Alton
Printed in the UK by Hobbs The Printer, Brunel Road, Totton, Hants

Introduction

Pira's *Visual Aid Kits* have been popular for many years but have previously only been available as sets of lecture notes and slides.

With the introduction of new editions of the *Kits*, we have taken the opportunity also to produce printed *Visual Guides* with the intention of fulfilling two additional objectives: to provide books which can be used in conjunction with the *Kits* (distributed to students or others attending lectures) or which can stand alone as learning aids.

Because the printing processes which developed through the ages were many and varied and because the provenance of some techniques still in use today is to be found in mediaeval printing technology, even basic explanations of the main processes are sometimes difficult to comprehend in a world which has in most other matters advanced many technical generations beyond the Industrial Revolution.

When considering how ink is put on paper in a production environment we have to offer explanations of chemical, mechanical, photographic and electronic processes. The varying approaches to the task can be confusing.

This is a case where a picture probably is worth a thousand words and that is the theory behind this publication. We hope the presentation of each picture facing its explanation is helpful.

Like the *Kits*, this is a basic primer for the uninitiated and the text varies little from the original lecture notes.

MB

1
Characteristics of the printing processes

THE PRINTING PROCESS

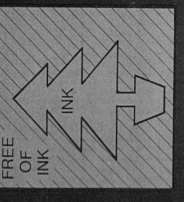

STAGE 1

STAGE 2

STAGE 3

FREE
OF
INK

INK

Three stages of printing

Printing is the reproduction of original material, be it text matter, illustrations or both, in ink on paper, board or other surfaces.

The illustration shows that printing can be divided into three stages:

1. The preparation of a surface on which the areas that must be inked can be separated from the areas that must remain uninked,
2. the application of ink,
3. transfer of the inked image to paper or other printing surfaces, usually by the application of pressure.

Thus, printing consists of an image surface preparation and image transfer process. All the operations needed to convert the original material to the prepared surface shown in Stage 1 are classified as *graphic reproduction*; Stages 2 and 3 – application of ink and image transfer – are classed as presswork.

PRINTING IMAGE CARRIER

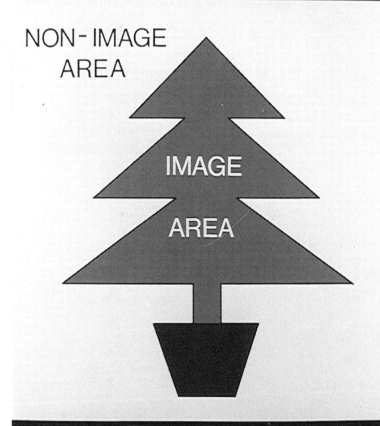

NON-IMAGE
AREA

IMAGE

AREA

The five main processes

If we set aside emergent – and, for the present, rather specialised – technologies such as electrophotograpic and ink jet printing, then there are five main printing processes – *offset lithography, gravure, flexography, screen process* and *letterpress*. The basic difference between them lies in the way image and non-image areas are separated on the printing image carrier.

The profile of the printing surface gives a characteristic appearance to prints from each process and imposes specific demands on the nature of the ink, the requirements of the printing stock and the construction of the printing press. Both directly and indirectly, it will determine which process is most suitable for a particular job of work.

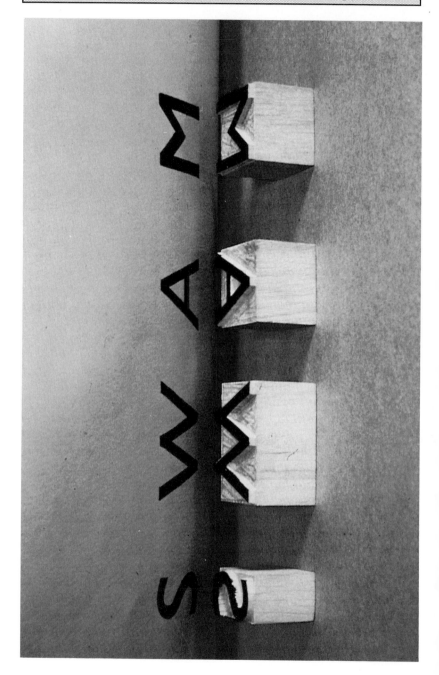

Relief printing

One of the most traditional methods of separating the image and non-image areas on the printing image carrier is by raising the image areas above the background.

If an inked roller is passed over the image carrier, it will ink the areas required to print, while leaving the background uninked. The inked image can now be transferred to paper by pressing the paper into contact with it.

Flexography uses this method of separating the image and non-image areas. It is classed as a *relief* process. The image carriers are made of either rubber or a special photopolymer and are flexible and deformable. The inks used for flexography are water- or solvent-based and so are very fluid, and thus known as *liquid inks*.

Letterpress is also a relief process although it differs from flexography in that it uses hard, non-deformable image carriers. These were traditionally made from hand carved wooden blocks or type-metal but today are more usually hard photopolymer. Letterpress inks are thick and sticky, commonly described as *paste inks*.

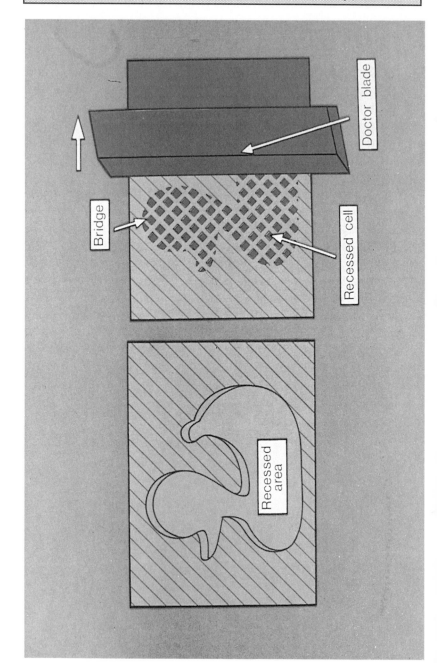

Gravure printing

This illustration shows a method of separating image and non-image areas that is the opposite of relief – the image areas are recessed below the surface of the image carrier.

Gravure uses this method of separating image and non-image areas. It is classed as an *intaglio* process.

On the left of the picture, the image has been etched or engraved into the background. If the surface is then flooded with a liquid ink and the ink removed from the background areas by a scraper or *doctor blade*, an inked image can be transferred to paper under pressure.

As it stands there would be some practical difficulties. Firstly, if the image were on a cylinder, ink would be thrown out of this large recessed area as the cylinder rotated. Secondly, the doctor blade would tend to dip into the recess, wiping ink out of it, and would probably become damaged.

To overcome these difficulties, the image areas are split up into tiny *cells* or *channels*, as shown on the right of the picture. The bridges or *lands* between the cells now act as a support for the doctor blade and ink is retained in the cells even when the cylinder rotates at high speed. The process of breaking the recessed area into tiny cells is called *screening*.

This process requires a free-flowing liquid ink which can be wiped easily from the non-image areas and will also flow out to cover over the bridges when the image is transferred to paper.

Lithographic printing

Raising or recessing image areas are obvious methods of separating them from the background, non-image areas. Separating them on a flat surface – the method used in lithography – requires a different approach.

Lithography is based on two principles:

1. The greasy ink used in lithography will transfer to any dry surface.
2. It will not readily mix with water.

On the left of the illustration, an inked roller is being passed over a flat metal sheet. The left side of the sheet is dry, and ink has transferred to it; the right hand side has been treated to make it water-accepting, and water has been applied to it. The water has flowed out, forming a thick film that adheres strongly to the metal, preventing the ink from contacting the metal surface. You can see that no ink is transferring.

On the right of the picture you can see in detail what happens when an inked roller is passed over a water repellent surface. Water will not spread over a repellent surface and wet it, but forms into small droplets. The inked roller is able to push these droplets aside, and transfer them to the dry metal surface.

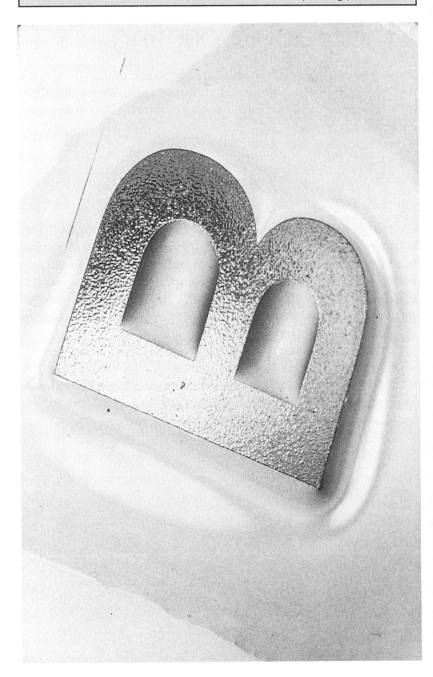

The planographic process

This illustration shows an inked image of a letter B on a lithographic plate. You can see that the image and the non-image areas are all on the same level. It is called a *planographic* process.

The non-image areas have been treated so that they are water-accepting. You can see a water film on the background, and in the loops of the letter B. This water film has protected these areas, and prevented them from inking-up.

The image areas are made to be water-repellent, so that water will not stick to them. Any water applied to the image areas would form droplets which would then be pushed aside onto the water-accepting, non-image areas of the plate.

When the lithographic plate is dry, both image and non-image areas will accept ink. When water is applied before the ink, the non-image areas accept the water and so reject the ink. The image areas repel the water and so accept ink.

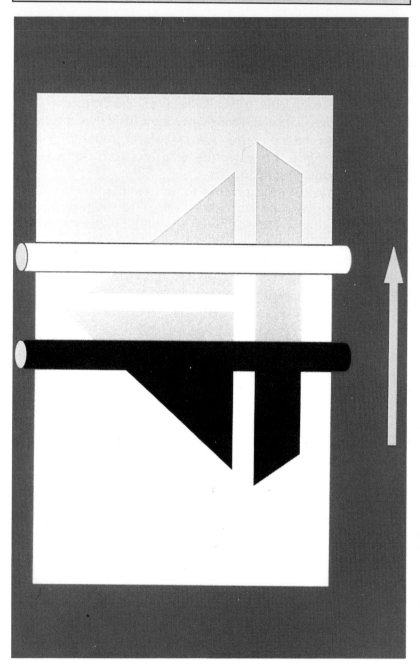

Use of water

As ink will transfer to any dry surface, a lithographic image carrier must be damped before it is inked.

This illustration shows a lithographic image carrier, or plate.

The image areas – the ship – have been made water repellent; the non-image areas water accepting.

A damping roller has been passed across the plate from left to right, leaving a water film adhering strongly to the non-image areas, but only water droplets on the image areas.

An inking roller is now passing across the plate from left to right, inking-up the image areas, while the non-image areas, protected by the water film, remain clear.

On a lithographic press, the plate must be damped during each revolution in order to maintain a water film over the non-image areas so that they are kept free of ink.

There is, in fact, a technique known as 'waterless litho' but this is not widely used as yet and we do not consider it here.

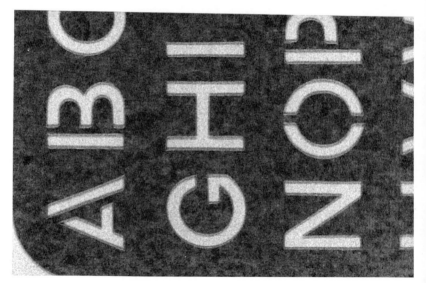

Printing from stencils

This slide shows a very simple method of separating image and non-image areas, by the use of a *stencil*. The stencils shown on the left of the picture are familiar to most people. The image areas have been cut out of the background, giving open areas through which ink can be applied to produce a print. A rather stylised reproduction is produced, due to the connecting links needed to hold the design together in the stencil.

Screen process printing using the basic principle of a stencil, has solved the problem of eliminating the connecting links by supporting all parts of the stencil on a fine mesh material stretched tightly across a frame, as shown on the right. Ink is poured into the frame, then spread across it and pushed through the open mesh areas with a *squeegee*.

Screen process is the only type of printing that prints through the image carrier, rather than from it.

LETTERPRESS & FLEXOGRAPHY

OFFSET LITHOGRAPHY

Metal

GRAVURE

Metal

SCREEN PROCESS

Paper

Summary of characteristics

This illustration indicates the basic characteristics of the image carriers for the main printing processes: relief; planographic; intaglio and stencil.

In flexography and letterpress, both relief processes, the printing surface is raised above the non-printing area. Flexography uses flexible, deformable relief plates made from either photopolymer or rubber. Letterpress uses hard, non-deformable photopolymer plates.

In lithography, a planographic process, the image and non-image areas are carried on the same surface of the image carrier. Each area has a different tolerance to water; the non-image areas accept water to act as a barrier to reject ink and the water repellent image areas reject water to leave them dry enough to accept the ink. An area that can be dampened with water will be made repellent to ink and is said to be desensitised, while an area that remains undampened and accepts ink is said to be sensitised.

In gravure, an intaglio process, the image areas are recessed below the surface of the image carrier. The image areas are screened (divided into tiny cells) to provide support for the doctor blade, which wipes the non-image areas clear of ink.

In screen printing, a stencil process, the image areas are the open areas of a stencil that is supported on a mesh material which is stretched tightly across a frame.

2
Letterpress printing

Photopolymer plates

This picture shows a typical letterpress image carrier. It is a photopolymer, relief plate.

A photopolymer is a material that changes on exposure to strong or ultra-violet (UV) rich light. A letterpress plate is produced by exposing the unexposed photopolymer to a UV light source through a film negative. (The image areas of the original are reproduced as clear areas on the negative.) The UV light hardens the photopolymer in the image areas, leaving the unexposed photopolymer soft enough to be washed away using a developer solution, often applied with a spray device and with brushes to help remove the photopolymer in the non-image areas.

Photopolymer letterpress plates are supplied with the light sensitive coating applied, very accurately to a given thickness, onto a flexible metal carrier sheet.

Once exposed and developed, the plate is mounted around the *plate cylinder* of the letterpress printing machine, ready for printing.

The older methods of producing a letterpress image carrier can still be found in use today and rely on the use of typemetal, wood or copper. These various image carriers were held in a metal frame called a *chase* which was then placed on the *flat bed* of the press reading for printing.

Label printing

Developments in lithography and flexography have led to a decline in the popularity of the letterpress printing process. However, it is still often used to print labels.

This picture shows a modern letterpress label printing machine.

The label material is unwound from a reel and passes through the press as a 'ribbon' or, to give it its correct name, a *web*. Similarly, presses using this system to feed the print substrate through them are called *web-fed* presses.

The press shown has the unwound reel of label paper on the left-hand side. The web then passes through a section that equalises the tensions within the reel to maintain control as it passes through the rest of the press. It also allows sideways adjustment of the web so that the image is printed in the correct position, or *in register* to the web.

The web then passes through the six letterpress units to be printed and on to a UV drying unit. There the inks are *cured* leaving them dry enough to allow the labels to be die-stamped and the waste label stock to be removed. The waste reel can be seen above the die-stamping unit to the right-hand side of the press with the finished labels re-reeled just below.

Each printing unit houses its own inking system comprising an *ink duct*, acting as a reservoir for the ink as well as feeding ink into the roller system in the required quantities. The rollers then supply a thin film of ink onto the raised surface of the photopolymer letterpress plate which is mounted on the plate cylinder. The label paper is printed by passing between the plate and the *impression cylinder*, the high impression causing the ink to transfer to the paper.

This particular press will print at web speeds of up to 120 metres per minute.

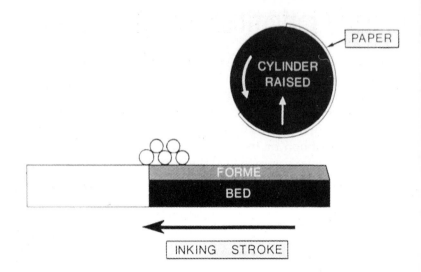

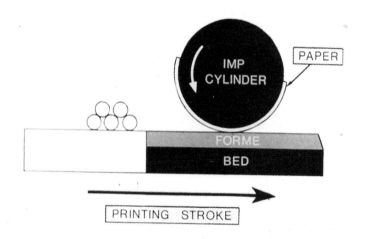

Flat bed cylinder presses

This picture shows two diagrams of an older letterpress printing method carried out using a *flat-bed cylinder press*. The *forme* is mounted on a flat bed, which moves backwards and forwards, while the paper is carried round an impression cylinder.

The diagram shows the kind of press called a *two-stroke*. At the top of the illustration, the forme is moving to the left, where it is linked up as it passes beneath the inking rollers. A sheet of paper is fed on chain grippers to the impression cylinder, which is at a higher level than the top of the forme.

In the bottom diagram, the inked forme has moved back to the right, and is passing beneath the impression cylinder. By the time the forme reaches it, the impression cylinder has also descended, so that it can now press the paper into contact with the forme. Ink is transferred from forme to paper as the forme passes under the impression cylinder.

The sheet of paper passes on to the delivery end of the machine, the cylinder now lifting again so that the forme can pass back beneath it, without touching it, on its way to be re-inked.

In this machine pressure is applied in narrow bands as the forme passes under the cylinder. Flat-bed presses are therefore capable of printing much larger sheets without requiring the impression power that would be needed by platen presses of the same size.

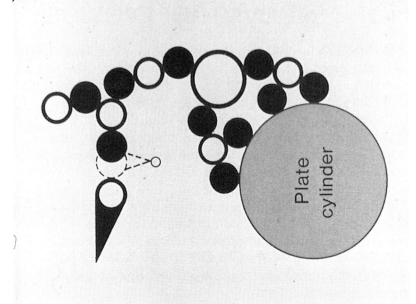

Letterpress inks

Letterpress inks consist basically of pigments dispersed in an oily, liquid vehicle. This picture shows the kind of ink used for letterpress printing: a thick, sticky semi-solid material which will stay where it is put on the raised image areas and not run down the sides of them and on to the background. These inks are described as paste inks.

Nevertheless, the ink has to be distributed and applied to the raised areas as a thin, even film. A long chain of rotating rollers, some of which also oscillate sideways, is needed to feed ink out of the duct on the press and break it down to a more fluid consistency so that it can be applied as an even film on the plate or type. Once at rest, the ink will thicken up again.

When printed, the ink must dry to a hard film as fast as possible, so that it will not smudge or smear. The quickest way of turning a liquid into a solid is by evaporation of a solvent – alcohol, for example. Unfortunately, a solvent cannot be used in these inks for it would evaporate on the roller train and the ink would dry before it reached the image carrier.

Letterpress inks dry by a process called *oxidation*. The oily vehicle absorbs oxygen from the air, turning gradually from a liquid through a gel-like state to a hard solid.

Driers can be added to speed up the process but, if it is accelerated too much, the ink will dry on the inking rollers. It must set rapidly to the gel state so that it will not set-off on to other sheets in the delivery pile, and this setting is assisted by absorbent materials, such as paper and board, which absorb some of the oily vehicle. Oxidation drying inks dry very slowly on non-absorbent materials such as plastics, films and metal foils, so letterpress is not particularly suited to printing on these materials. Further, because the inks take some time to dry hard, even on paper and board, some time must be allowed to elapse before converting operations can be done.

3
Lithography

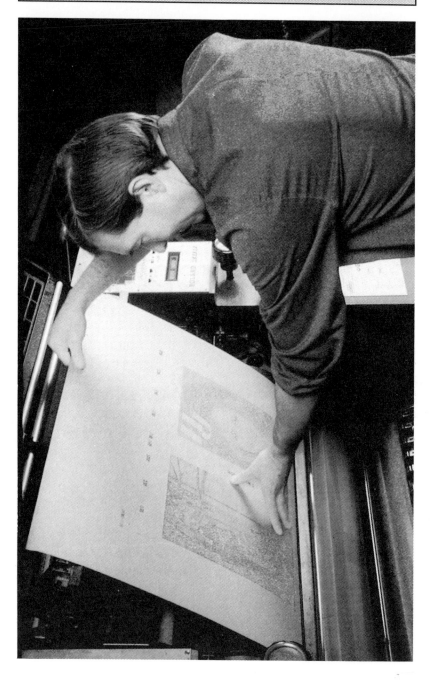

Lithographic plates

This illustration shows a lithographic plate (image carrier) being fitted onto the plate cylinder of a lithographic press.

Each lithographic plate carries one image. For multi-colour work a number of plates will be required, each one carrying the correct image areas for each colour required.

You will notice that the image and non-image areas of the plate lie in the same plane, the difference between them being their ability to accept or reject water. The most common material used for lithographic plates is aluminium as it naturally accepts water, although plates made from treated polyester or paper are available and are usually used for shorter run lengths.

There are a number of different ways of imaging a lithographic plate, the most common being the *pre-sensitised* plate. The plates consist of an aluminium substrate of accurate thickness, coated mostly with a light-sensitive photopolymer. Coatings are manufactured to be light-sensitive in one of two ways: by hardening or by changing to become soluble in a developing solution. The coatings that harden are exposed through a film negative and are called *negative working* and the coatings that become soluble are exposed through a film positive and so are called *positive working*.

Other plate imaging systems include the *chemical transfer* or *CT* plate which uses reflected light from an original to expose a light sensitive coating applied to a paper carrier. The plate and paper carrier are then developed in contact with one another to leave silver halide crystals deposited in the image areas of the plate. Chemical transfer plates are used widely for small offset, short run work.

Photo-direct plates are more light sensitive than pre-sensitised plates, using silver halide coatings. They are exposed to reflected light from the original in a special camera platemaking unit.

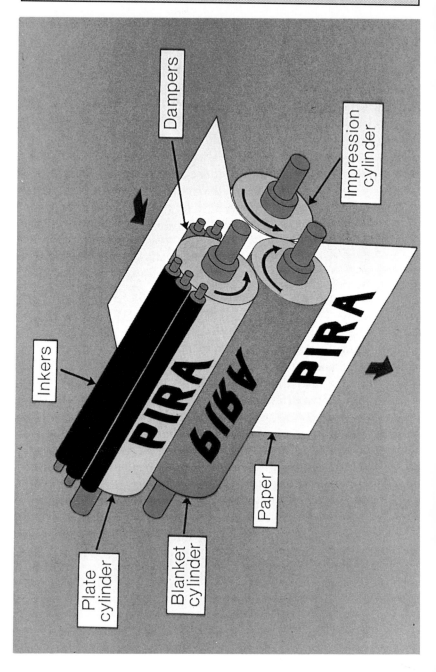

The offset principle

We have looked at lithographic plates, but the printing process is called offset lithography.

This picture explains why it is called *offset*.

Offset lithography is not a direct printing process. The lithographic plate, which is fitted around the plate cylinder, does not print directly on the substrate but 'offsets' the image onto a rubber *blanket* attached to the cylinder, thus fundamentally changing the nature of the process. The image area which is *right reading*, as shown by the PIRA, becomes *wrong reading* on the blanket cylinder and then right reading onto the printing paper/substrate.

The offset process greatly enhances the quality of the image and allows the image on the plate to be protected from abnormal roughness, thus considerably extending the life of the plate.

The great advantage of the offset principle is the ability of the process to print very fine halftones and illustrations while retaining optimum colour.

Lithography is a flexible process; it produces a wide variety of printing ranging from stationery through to very high quality magazine and brochure work. It has become popular with many daily newspapers as it produces a good quality print on low quality papers.

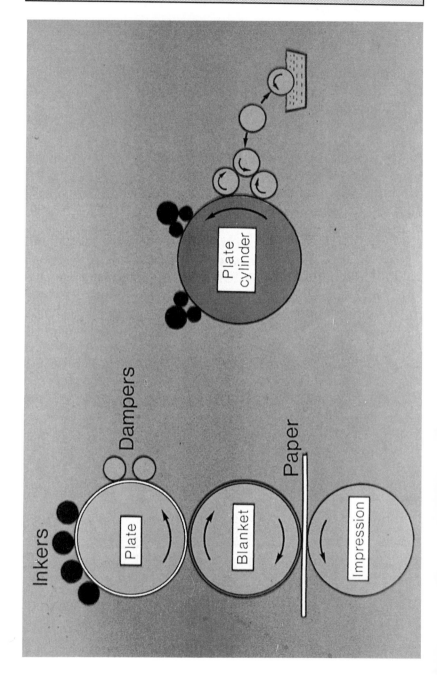

Printing units and ink

On the left is a diagram of one printing unit of an offset lithographic press.

You can see that it has three main cylinders: the plate cylinder; blanket cylinder; and impression cylinder. The inked image is transferred from the plate to the blanket and then on to the paper. The substrate passes between the blanket and impression cylinders, but never contacts the plate.

Remember that plates must be damped before they are inked, and kept damp throughout the run, to desensitise the non-image areas. You can see in the picture that the plate passes under a set of *dampers* before it passes under the plate inkers.

The damping unit (right of the picture) applies an aqueous solution – called a *fountain solution* – to the plate at each revolution. Fountain solutions are mainly water, with small quantities of additives to enhance the water-receptivity of non-image areas, prevent the growth of bacteria or fungi, and keep the solution at the correct acidity.

Inks for lithography have to be attracted to and remain on the image areas and mix with the fountain solution to form a water in ink emulsion. They therefore tend to be tacky.

Lithographic inks differ from other paste inks in that they have to split twice: from plate to blanket and from blanket to paper. Therefore a thin ink film is deposited. To maintain the required colour strength or *saturation*, litho inks are more highly pigmented.

Inks used for lithography dry by a number of means:

1. By oxidation, which on some presses can be accelerated by warming the sheets under infrared lamps
2. by curing special inks under a UV rich light source,
3. by heatset, drying the inks by passing the printed web through a hot, turbulent air, oven which dries the inks, which are then *set* by cooling the web,
4. by using an absorbent paper and relying on the ink being absorbed into it: *coldset* drying.

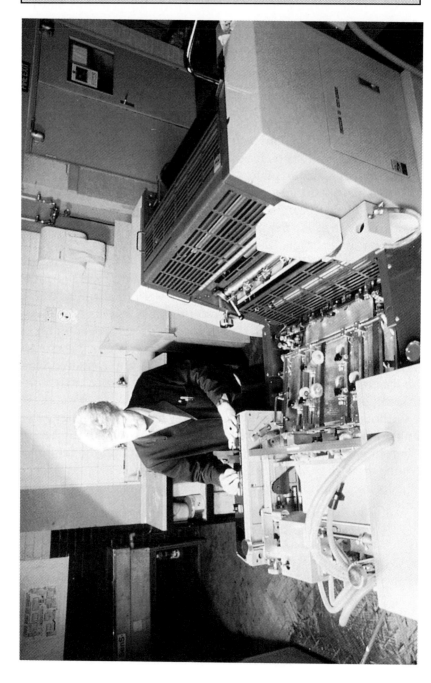

Small offset

This shows a small offset press.

Paper is fed into the press from the feeder on the left. The sheet to be printed is fed along the supporting *feed board* which controls the position and passage of the sheet through the press. The paper is then fed down between the blanket and an impression cylinder which is guarded and appears on the right of the press.

The damping unit can be seen above the feed board to the right, alongside the bottle holding the damping solution, which acts as a filler to the reservoir within the system.

Small offset is a common application of the lithographic process, using presses capable of printing on sheets of paper and light card up to approximately A3 (420 x 297 mm) in size. These presses normally have one printing unit and are capable of printing only a single colour per pass of the sheets through the press. More sophisticated presses are also available, with four or five printing units giving the press multi-colour ability. Many press manufacturers offer a secondary unit to attach to single colour presses to facilitate crash numbering, perforating and, in some cases, second colour printing.

Developments in control systems have introduced small offset presses with the ability to print pre-set run lengths and change plates automatically.

Small offset presses are normally used by print shops, implant printers and general jobbing printers. They are usually employed to print short run work of up to approximately 5,000 copies, using only one or two colours.

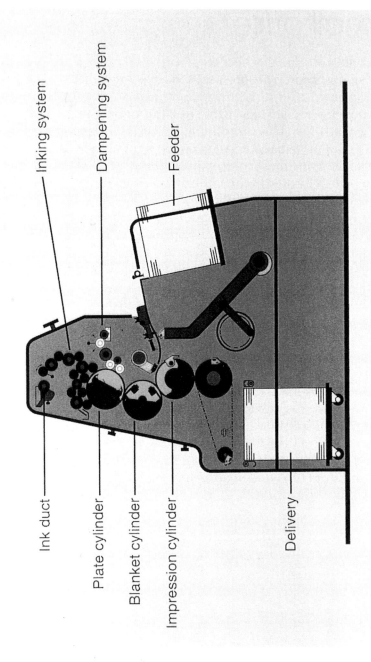

Inking system

Dampening system

Feeder

Ink duct

Plate cylinder

Blanket cylinder

Impression cylinder

Delivery

Press cylinders

Here we show a cross-sectional diagram of a small offset press.

The printing unit can be clearly seen with the three main cylinders arranged vertically through the middle of the press. The top cylinder carries the plate and is therefore called the plate cylinder. The plate surface runs in contact with the dampening and inking systems, so that both fountain solution and ink are applied as the cylinder rotates.

The inked image on the plate is then transferred, under impression, to the surface of the blanket, which is held onto the surface of the middle cylinder, the blanket cylinder.

Finally, the inked image is supported by the lower cylinder, the impression cylinder.

The inking system, at the top of the unit, consists of 15 rollers fed with ink from the ink duct, which acts as a reservoir for the ink. It also provides a means to control the amount of ink fed into the system, using keys, so that ink is fed corresponding to image requirements.

The damping system is shown to the right of the plate cylinder and consists of six rollers. The damping system simply feeds fountain solution from the trough or fountain to the plate surface.

The press is sheet-fed and so has a feed stack of paper to the right of the print unit and a delivery stack below.

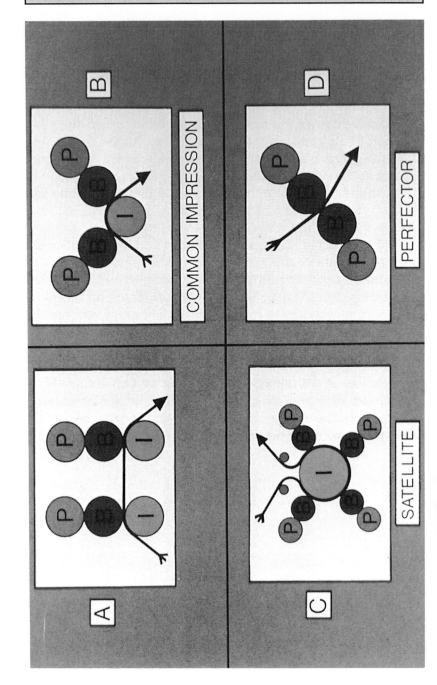

Four types of press

To print more than one colour on one pass through a press, a unit would be needed for each colour. Two units side-by-side are shown in diagram A. Four or six units like this would take up a great deal of space.

More compact presses can be made by using the arrangement shown in diagram B. One impression cylinder is used to support the paper which is being printed from two blankets at the same time. Presses built on this principle are called *common impression presses*.

By going one stage further, one large *common impression drum* can be used to support the paper being printed from four blankets (diagram C). This arrangements is called a *satellite unit*, and is used on web offset, not sheet-fed, presses and produces high quality process printing.

All these arrangements print on one side of the paper only. As the impression cylinder does not transfer an image but merely supports the paper, both sides of the paper can be printed at the same time by replacing it with another blanket cylinder (diagram D). Here the blanket cylinder of one unit acts as an impression cylinder for the other unit. This type of arrangement is known as a *blanket-to-blanket perfector*.

Whatever the arrangements of units, each plate cylinder must have its own inking and damping system.

Colour presses

This shows a large four-colour sheet-fed press, using the common impression principle to print on board for packaging. In the background is the board as delivered; two pallets have been unwrapped, and the board is ready to be fed to the press.

The board is fed through the two towers of the press, each containing a two-colour, common impression printing unit. The sheets, printed with four colours, can be seen being delivered at the end of the press nearest the camera.

On colour work, the ink/water balance is critical for the production of high quality, consistent prints. Colour variation throughout the run can be caused by an imbalance of the ink and water feed. Online computer-aided quality control systems can assist in maintaining ink/water balance, and help regulate the level of printed output.

To maximise plate life, plate inkers and dampers must be set uniformly. Pressure between the blanket and the plate must be consistent with good ink transfer, and the cylinders must be packed to the right diameters to rotate in unison, so avoiding slippage and maintaining image size. Excess pressure on the plate will cause plate wear and shorten its life.

Lithography relies on the maintenance of the ink/water balance which is fundamental in achieving correct colour and image quality.

Web presses

Sheet-fed presses, as their name suggests, print separate sheets of paper taken from a stack. Each sheet is fed through the printing unit and on to the delivery stack using a series of grippers.

On web presses, continuous webs of paper are fed to the printing units from a reel held in a reel-stand.

Reels of paper on the reel-stands in the basement are fed up to four blanket-to-blanket perfecting units on the floor above. The press is operated from the console in the centre of the picture; two of the printing units can be seen to the left of this console. After printing, the webs are brought together, pass through a folding unit in the centre, and the complete newspapers then pass straight on to a delivery belt which convey them to the dispatch floor. One of the conveyors can be seen to the right of the console and a complete newspaper is being checked to the right of it.

Web offset presses tend to be custom-built to suit the number of pages of monochrome and colour required, colour pages sometimes being reproduced in a satellite unit.

Whereas sheet-fed presses print on average 8,000 - 10,000 sheets per hour, with a maximum of 15,000, web presses can print in the region of 40,000 complete copies per hour.

Web offset is used widely for provincial and daily newspapers, magazines, catalogues and book work. As stated earlier, the offset principle makes it possible to print fine tonal work and even solids on a range of paper stocks as the offset blanket deforms itself into any irregularities in the paper surface.

4
Gravure printing

Gravure cylinders

This picture shows a gravure printing image carrier, a copper plated steel cylinder that is etched or engraved in the image areas and chrome plated, so making it durable enough to withstand very long runs of several million. It is positioned in the ink duct of a gravure press.

Gravure can be classified by the two types of cell that are etched or engraved into the cylinder. They are *conventional*, where the cells remain constant in area but vary in depth; or *halftone*, where the cells vary in area as well as depth.

The most commonly used method to produce the recessed image is to engrave each individual cell using a diamond tipped *stylus*. The recessed image area is produced by scanning reflection copy to create a digitised signal which drives the stylus into and out of the rotating copper plated cylinder, creating inverted pyramid shaped cells, varying in depth and area. The cylinder is then chromium plated for durability.

Traditionally there were many stages in producing a gravure cylinder. Following copper plating of the steel or iron cylinder, a light sensitive, acid *resist* was applied to it. The design was then transferred to it photographically and broken up into tiny cells using a gravure screen. The resist was then washed away in the image areas and then the cylinder surface was etched using a series of varying strength acids. The resist prevented the cell walls from being etched away so that a screened, recessed image area remained.

Because the cylinder rotates in the ink duct, and a long chain of inking rollers is not required, a fluid, solvent-based ink can be used. This dries in seconds by evaporation, aided by a heated drying tunnel. Gravure inks are therefore suitable for printing at high speed on non-absorbent materials such as plastic films and metal foils.

The intensity and cost of the cylinder preparation makes gravure more economic for medium to long run work – and it is particularly suited to long run multi-colour printing.

Gravure cells

This picture shows a microphotograph of the conventionally etched cylinder. Ink is held in the cells, while the cell walls or lands act as a support for the doctor blade.

The cells are about .127 mm in diameter, and vary in depth from approximately .001 to .04 mm. The shallow cells will print light tones, whereas the deeper cells holding more ink will produce darker tones. The ink held in the deeper cells flows out to cover the bridges and gives a continuous print in the solid areas. This continuous tone effect is produced by both conventionally etched and electronically engraved cells. Different tone values are re-produced by the varying depth of the cells.

In most printing processes, where pictures have to be repro-duced, a halftone screen is used to break the image down into a dot structure to create the illusion of tone. The gravure process pro-duces the closest to a continuous tone effect.

The conventional gravure process, however, has a major drawback. Continued contact with the doctor blade erodes the shallow depth of the highlight cell, resulting in fine detail being lost in these areas. In an attempt to overcome this problem the halftone method of producing cells was developed, where the cells vary in area as well as depth.

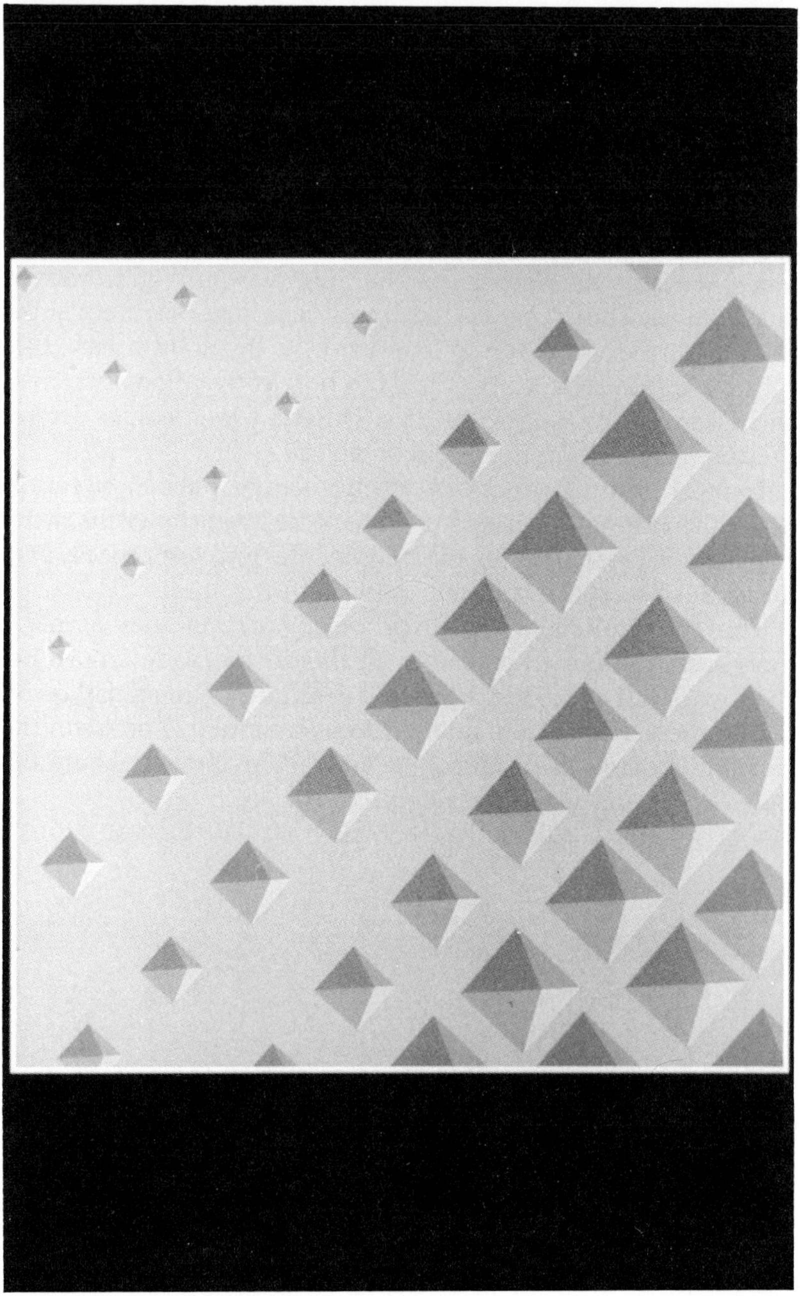

Engraving cylinders

This illustration represents an engraved gravure cylinder surface which has been imaged using an electromechanical process.

Each individual cell is engraved into the copper surface of the cylinder using a machine called a Helio Klischograph. The machine scans the copy mounted onto a cylinder which is rotated at the same speed as the gravure cylinder to be imaged. The scanning head, containing a light source and a photocell, moves across the copy cylinder as it is rotated. As it does so, the light sources illuminate the copy and are reflected into the photocell. The varying intensity of the reflected light, caused by the different images of the copy, are transformed into electrical signals and passed to a computer within the machine by the photocell. The scanned information is processed by the computer and output to the engraving head, which engraves the cells individually, using a diamond tipped stylus. The stylus is pyramid shaped and so produces a four sided, inverted, pyramid-shaped cell, the depth and area depending upon how deep the stylus cuts into the copper. When the cylinder surface has been completely engraved, it is then chrome plated to increase its durability.

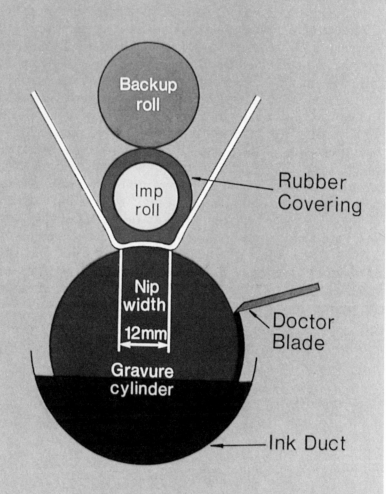

Backup roll

Imp roll

Rubber Covering

Nip width

12mm

Doctor Blade

Gravure cylinder

Ink Duct

Gravure printing units

This is a diagram of one unit of a gravure press.

The gravure cylinder rotates in a very fluid ink contained in the ink reservoir. As the cylinder leaves the ink reservoir it carries a thick film of ink on its surface. This layer is wiped off the surface by the doctor blade, leaving ink only in the recessed cells. The doctor blade reciprocates across the cylinder helping to spread any wear. The pressure of the blade must remain constant and there are various methods of ensuring that this is achieved, such as spring or hydraulic controlled systems.

The pressure needed to transfer ink from the cells/channels to paper is applied by a rubber covered impression cylinder. On publication presses, where the gravure cylinders may be up to 2,500 mm long, a steel back-up roller rides on top of the impression cylinder to provide extra rigidity.

After printing, the paper runs through a drying chamber where the solvent is reclaimed.

The only power driven cylinder in the unit is the gravure cylinder, all the others being driven by contact with the gravure cylinder or by the moving web of paper. Thus in gravure, unlike offset lithography, the cylinders are not geared together. Within limits, therefore, presses can be built to accommodate cylinders of different diameter.

Gravure colour

The gravure process is used to print a wide range of products including long run and multi-colour magazine work, mail order catalogues, stamps and various packaging and security materials.

The picture shows a thirteen unit multi-colour gravure press.

Four colours can be printed on both sides of one web of paper, while four colours one side, and black on the other are printed on a second web. The gravure cylinders can range up to 3 m in length, each printing 24 pages or more. A magazine of up to 96 pages is possible, with 72 pages in full colour, at a speed of 20,000 magazines per hour.

Good quality printing can be done at high speed on relatively cheap uncoated papers. Coated papers are used for quality magazines and mail-order catalogues.

All gravure presses are rotary and use reel-fed systems.

The press is operated from a console mid-way down the gangway. Ink is pumped up from underground storage tanks outside the building. The square tanks at each side of each unit house automatic viscosity control equipment.

Package printing

This illustration shows a gravure press used for printing on non-paper surfaces such as plastic, film or foil.

In this instance, the press is printing four colours on ICI's 'Melinex' brand of polyester film, subsequently made up into packets for boil-in-the-bag fish. The ink, sandwiched between two films, is protected from damage, and cannot contact the food. The inner polythene layer allows the bag to be heat-sealed. Presses for package printing are available in a range of different web widths, down to as narrow as 50 mm.

Gravure is an ideal process for this type of package printing. The solvent-based inks can be formulated to key on to a wide variety of films, and low-odour inks are available for food packaging. The rapid drying of solvent-based inks makes in-line converting operations possible. Recycling techniques ensure maximum use of the gravure ink and reduce toxicity. After printing, webs can be slit, embossed, cut and creased, all in one continuous operation. A gravure unit can be used to apply adhesive or varnish instead of ink.

The solvent-based inks are also useful for printing on plastics for uses other than packaging, such as decorative laminates, floor tiles, wallpapers and plastic-coated shelf papers.

5
Flexography

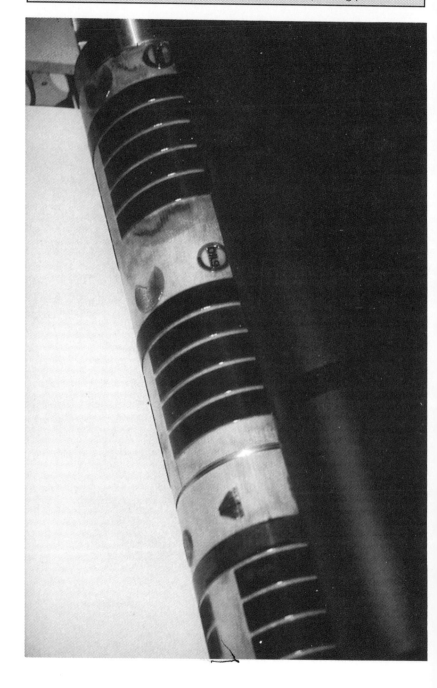

Flexographic plates

Flexography is a relief printing process, and uses an image carrier that is deformable and flexible.

This picture shows a photopolymer flexographic plate mounted on a plate cylinder. It is a relief printing plate, having the image areas raised above the non-image areas.

Relief photopolymer plates are produced by exposing them to strong UV light, using a film negative to define the image and non-image areas. The unexposed photopolymer is removed using a developing fluid and soft brushes housed within a plate developing unit. An all-over exposure to the UV light then ensures all of the photopolymer is solidified. Finally the plates are de-tacked to remove the stickiness of the photopolymer.

The plates are then mounted onto the plate cylinder of the press using double-sided adhesive, reading for printing.

Recent developments in photopolymer technology, ink technology and press design have led to increased use of flexography. Fast evaporating liquid inks can print multi-colour work successfully onto plastic films for packaging use.

The process is also used to print newspapers, again including colour work, with some success, its advantage over the more commonly found offset lithographic applications being increased colour strength and reduced waste.

Flexographic plates can also be made from rubber. They are produced using a mould or matrix which itself is moulded from an original metal or hard photopolymer relief plate. Any number of plates can be produced using the matrix. These rubber plates are commonly called *rubber stereos*.

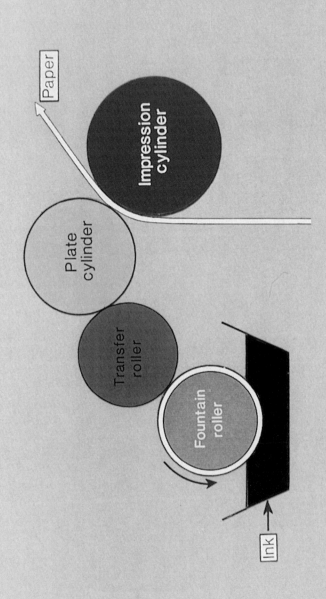

Flexographic printing units

This diagram shows the printing unit of a flexographic press.

The ink is contained in the ink duct or fountain. Notice that there are only two inking rollers: a rubber covered fountain roller which rotates in the fountain, carrying ink up to a transfer or forme roller, which in turn inks the plates or stereos mounted on the plate cylinder. The transfer roller is called an *anilox*, and is engraved or etched with an overall pattern of small cells, which act as ink-carrying reservoirs. The amount of ink carried to the plate by the anilox roller is controlled by the number and size of these cells. Ceramic anilox rollers and doctor blades have been introduced for greater control of ink systems. Water-based and UV cured inks have been introduced to enhance image quality.

Because the inking system has been reduced to two rollers only, it is possible to use fast drying solvent-based inks, similar to those used in gravure. Thus the process is eminently suitable for packaging work on non-absorbent plastics, films and foils.

The function of the impression cylinder is to support the web of printing stock and bring it into contact with the photopolymer plate with just enough pressure to transfer ink from the raised areas to the web.

Remember that the ink is very fluid, and the plate has a raised image area, so there is a pronounced tendency for the ink to be squeezed out round the edges of the image. This gives a distinctive rim around the printed image, called *squash*. It is essential to print with the lowest possible pressure to minimise the effects of squash and produce good quality prints. Cushion back adhesives are used to reduce the effect of plate imperfections, and enable minimum impression to be achieved more easily, so relieving the inherent characteristic of squash.

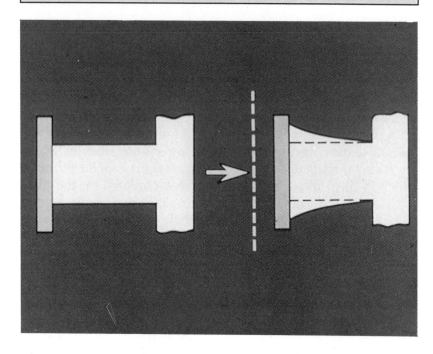

Flexographic squash

This shows the causes of squash in more detail.

On the left of the illustration is an example of increased squash. You can see how the ink has been squeezed out at the edges of the plastic or rubber plate, giving a distinctive rim of ink separated from the main body of the print. On fine type, the loops of the letter would fill-in. Plastic photopolymer plates have a limited compressibility and are therefore less prone to pressure squash than conventional rubber stereos. However, the nature of the ink and image surface allows a minimum level of excess ink to form a rim around the main body of the image.

The right hand side of the picture shows the effect of the compressibility of a rubber stereo. This means it will distort under pressure but will not change in volume. If the top plate in the diagram is taken to represent the printing stock then, under impression, the rubber will distort as shown on the bottom right of the picture, causing the familiar enlargement of the dot or printed character. When pressure is released, the rubber returns to its original dimensions, but will distort again each time pressure is applied.

Flexography has traditionally produced excellent line and solid work in strong, vibrant colours. In recent times, with the improvement in plate technology, the quality of halftone work and four-colour printing has widened the appeal of this process. To limit squash, and maintain the correct impression over the whole printing surface area, the cylinders and plates need to be made to close tolerances. The ink supply would require to be controlled using an anilox roller, the surface of which is cleared of ink using a doctor blade and not just the interference of the transfer roller.

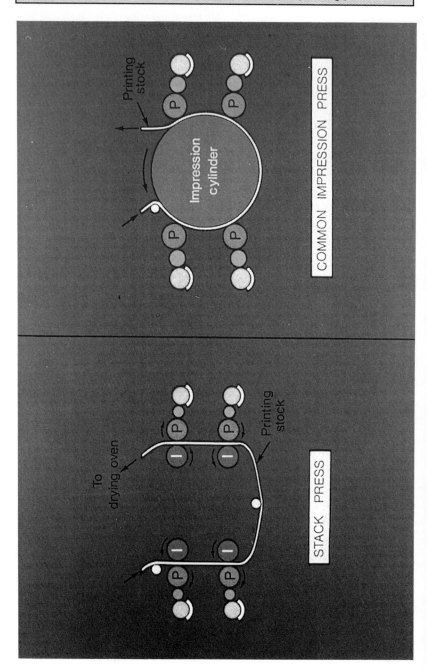

COMMON IMPRESSION PRESS

Printing stock

Impression cylinder

STACK PRESS

To drying oven

Printing stock

Flexographic press types

Flexographic presses can be classified broadly into three types: *stack*; *common impression*; and *in-line*.

On the left is a diagram of a stack press. Printing units are stacked one above the other on one or both sides of a main drive frame. The web to be printed is fed through each colour unit in turn, and then into a drying tunnel. One or more colour units can be reversed so that both sides of the web can be printed. On the right of the illustration is a common impression cylinder press. Instead of each printing unit having its own impression cylinder, the units are grouped round one large impression drum.

It is more difficult to dry inks between units on this kind of press, but it is easier to maintain good register between colours, as the web is held in contact with the drum. Thin films that wrinkle and stretch under very light tension are difficult to web without support over long distances.

All kinds of material are printed on both types of press, but the common impression press is the more suitable for thin stretchable films, cloth and thin papers.

In-line presses have the colour units arranged one after another in a line, the web feeding horizontally through each unit in turn. These presses are most suitable for thicker materials and multiple operations and techniques.

The improved quality of the flexographic image and press have made it suitable not only for packaging but also for book printing, daily newspapers and comics. The fast drying inks permit high-speed printing and in-line converting operations such as label or form sheeting and bag making. It is used for the printing of paper towels and toilet tissues, paper bags, plastic carrier bags, multi-wall and other heavy duty sacks, corrugated boards, as well as a wide range of packaging films and foils.

6
Screen printing

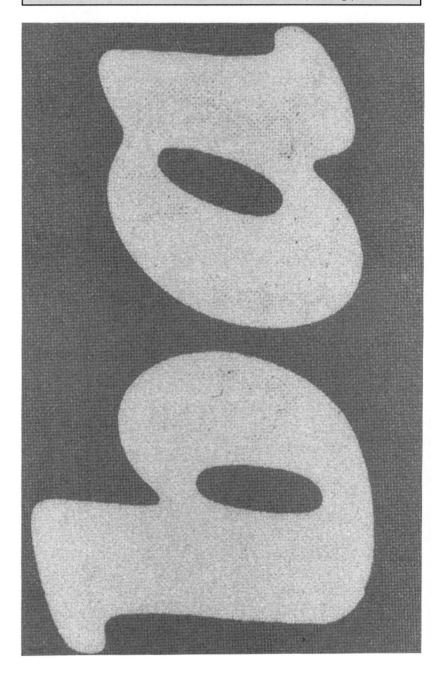

Screen process image carriers

This shows the essential features of the image carrier. You can see that open areas of a stencil form the image areas and that the stencil is supported on a mesh. This enables images such as the centres of the letter 'b' and 'a' to be printed without the need for linking bridges to hold the non-image area of the stencil. During printing, ink is forced through the open areas of the mesh using a flexible blade called a squeegee.

Meshes are made from dimensionally stable materials including nylon, polyester and stainless steel and are stretched tightly across a frame. The thickness of ink film that can be printed is largely controlled by the thickness of the mesh material and various types of mesh are available for different kinds of work.

Stencils can be produced manually or photographically, the simplest method being hand cut stencils. These are produced by cutting the non-image areas out of a special stencil film which is then attached (normally by ironing) to the mesh. Halftone and fine detail work is reproduced using either *direct* or *indirect* stencils. A direct stencil is produced by applying a light sensitive coating onto the mesh, which is then exposed to UV light through a film positive. The exposed coating hardens to produce the stencil and the unexposed areas are developed away leaving open, image areas. Indirect stencils work in a similar way except the photopolymer is exposed and developed out on a carrier sheet before being applied to the mesh.

The screen process method

Screen printing is essentially an automated printing process. However, semi-automatic and hand printing methods are still used.

The picture shows the image carrier being used in an automatic press.

In all cases, a working supply of ink must be placed at one end of the screen. To produce a print, the screen first rises so that the substrate (material) can be fed into position beneath it. The screen is then lowered, and the squeegee blade draws ink across the stencil, forcing it through the open areas of the mesh to produce the printed image.

The pressure, angle and sharpness of the blade will affect the thickness of ink printed. After printing, the screen lifts and the printed substrate emerges, or is removed, from beneath it.

Screen printing is less dependent on sophisticated systems than other print processes. The frame and stencil act as an ink reservoir for a working supply of ink, so no complex independent inking systems are required.

Further, the only pressure on the printing substrate is that of the squeegee as it passes across the screen.

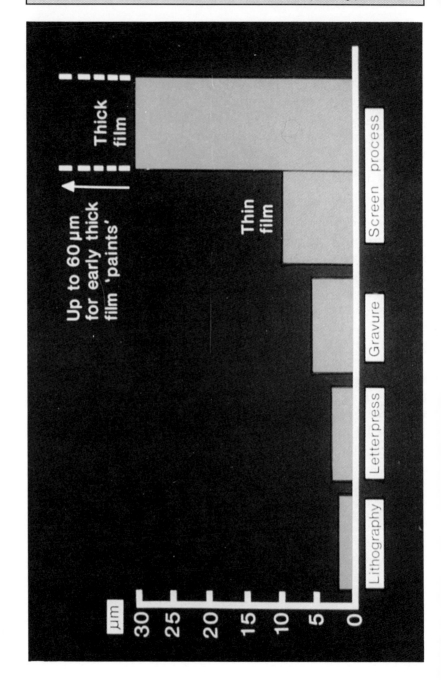

Ink thicknesses

This illustration compares the thickness of the ink films printed by screen process with those of other printing processes.

Screen process inks deposit a layer of film 30 times thicker than that of lithographic inks and six times thicker than that of gravure.

These inks may dry by oxidation for conventional surfaces, but with some substrates the process of drying will be extended and will require the material to be racked.

These 'buttery', opaque inks are ideal for printing bold and solid colours well suited for posters and advertising displays. Screen printing can deposit an ink on most surfaces, including those that are rigid and flexible. Screen also prints on a range of textiles.

Recent developments include the introduction of water-based inks, which reduce toxicity. Improved stencil production has also enhanced the quality of image for screen printing and it is now possible to print fine details, four-colour process printing and complex images.

The dot structure for halftone printing still remains less defined than for offset or gravure, but improvements in mesh types have increased the resolution considerably.

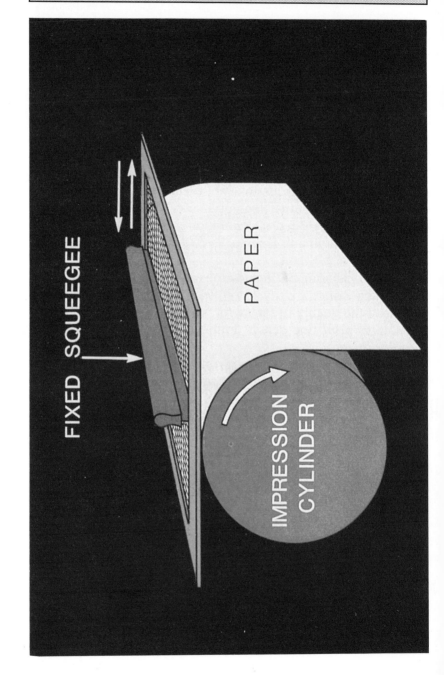

Screen process cylinder presses

This shows a diagram of another type of press – the *cylinder press*.

In a cylinder press, the squeegee remains stationary during the printing cycle, while the screen moves backwards and forwards.

The printing unit consists of an impression cylinder, a carriage for the screen, and a squeegee. The stock to be printed is clamped by grippers at the leading edge of the cylinder and held firmly to its surface by vacuum. As the cylinder and screen move in unison, the fixed squeegee pushes the ink through the mesh on to the substrate being carried between the cylinder and the screen to produce the print.

Fully automatic flat-bed and cylinder presses are used for long run work. Speeds vary according to the type of work and machine, with cylinders generally being faster. The printing of rigid materials is not possible on most cylinder presses.

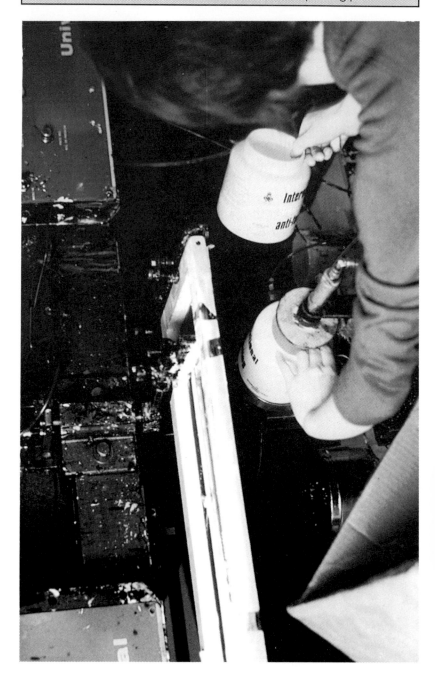

Versatility

Screen process is used extensively for industrial and packaging printing on a range of pre-fabricated articles – containers, bottles, knobs and dials, equipment and machinery, sport and leisure holdalls, toys, and a range of clothing including T-shirts and designer jackets. Many articles are printed on semi-automatic presses, and there are few limitations on size or shape. Objects ranging from oil drums down to pens and lipstick cases can be dealt with.

In the picture, polythene containers are being printed on a semi-automatic press. The principle is that of the cylinder press, with the container taking the place of the cylinder. The squeegee is fixed, while the screen moves to and fro. A gear mechanism turns the container in a reciprocating action in time with the screen. Thin-walled bottles are inflated to give a stable printing surface.

Special screens and jigs can be designed to print on peculiar shaped objects, such as cups with handles, ovals, tapers or recessed panels. Print heads are available that can be bolted on to and over any automated process line. In come cases printing may form part of a completely integrated production line from polythene bottle manufacture to filled bottles. A complete line would comprise a blow-moulding machine, pre-treatment unit, printing units and a filling, capping and packing station.

Screen process can compete in many areas with other printing processes. Its ability to print very thick films and to print on any shape and size of article also give it areas of application outside the range of other processes.